What Makes Your Body WORK?

Gill Arbuthnott

ILLUSTRATED BY
Marc Mones

Crabtree Publishing Company
www.crabtreebooks.com

Crabtree Publishing Company
www.crabtreebooks.com
1-800-387-7650

Published in Canada
Crabtree Publishing
616 Welland Avenue
St. Catharines, ON
L2M 5V6

Published in the United States
Crabtree Publishing
PMB 59051
350 Fifth Ave, 59th Floor
New York, NY 10118

Published by Crabtree Publishing Company in 2016

For Isis and Orla
(but maybe not just yet!)

Author: Gill Arbuthnott

Project coordinator: Kathy Middleton

Editor: Crystal Sikkens

Proofreader: Janine Deschenes

Prepress technician: Tammy McGarr

Print and production coordinator:
   Margaret Amy Salter

Science Consultant: Shirley Duke

First published in 2015 by A & C Black, an imprint of Bloomsbury Publishing Plc
Copyright © 2015 A & C Black

Printed in Canada/022016/MA20151130

Library and Archives Canada Cataloguing in Publication

Arbuthnott, Gill, author
      What makes your body work? / Gill Arbuthnott ; Marc Mones, illustrator.

(Drawn to science, illustrated guides to key science concepts)
Includes index.
ISBN 978-0-7787-2241-0 (bound).--
ISBN 978-0-7787-2249-6 (paperback)

      1. Human physiology--Juvenile literature. I. Mones, Marc, illustrator II. Title.

QP37.A72 2016   j612   C2015-907106-2

Library of Congress Cataloging-in-Publication Data

Names: Arbuthnott, Gill, author. | Mones, Marc, illustrator.
Title: What makes your body work? / Gill Arbuthnott ; illustrated by
   Marc Mones.
Description: Crabtree Publishing Company, 2016. | Series: Drawn to
   science : illustrated guides to key science concepts | Includes index.
Identifiers: LCCN 2015042098| ISBN 9780778722410 (reinforced library
   binding : alk. paper) | ISBN 9780778722496 (pbk. : alk. paper)
Subjects: LCSH: Human body--Juvenile literature. | Human
   physiology--Juvenile literature.
Classification: LCC QP37 .A726 2016 | DDC 612--dc23
LC record available at http://lccn.loc.gov/2015042098

Contents

The Human Body

The brain

The eyes

The ears

The nose
and tongue

The skin

The skeletal
system

The lungs

The heart

The digestive
system

The muscle
system

Introduction

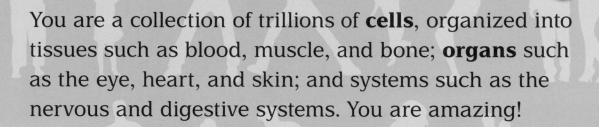

You are a collection of trillions of **cells**, organized into tissues such as blood, muscle, and bone; **organs** such as the eye, heart, and skin; and systems such as the nervous and digestive systems. You are amazing!

How do all of these parts work? What can they do? This book takes you on a tour around your own body, and shows you how to carry out simple experiments. These experiments will show us how the human body is an incredible, living machine!

Read on and find out...
What makes your
body work?

The Skin

The skin is the largest organ of the body. If you could take it off and spread it out flat, it would measure about 21.5 square feet (2 square meters). That's about the same area as the mattress of a large single bed.

Skin gets worn away very quickly, because it is constantly rubbing against your clothes. As a result, your body is always making new skin cells. The old ones are probably lying about your house. In fact, most of what you think is dust is actually dead skin! You lose about one million skin cells every day. All of your skin is replaced once every four to five weeks, but you don't notice because, unlike a snake, you don't do it all at once.

Scars

If your skin is replaced so often, then why don't scars disappear? And what about tattoos—shouldn't they vanish, too?

The answer is that the layer of skin that is replaced is the *outer layer*, called the **epidermis**. Scars are caused by damage to a *deeper layer* of skin called the **dermis**. Tattoo ink also sits on the dermis. This deeper layer of skin isn't replaced in the same way as the outer layer.

Your skin is essential for a variety of reasons. It's sensitive to touch, pressure, temperature, and pain, and it is also very important in controlling body temperature. Read on to discover more...

Temperature sensitivity

Your skin is very sensitive to temperature. This doesn't mean that you can put your finger in a glass of water and tell exactly what temperature it is! However, if you dip your finger into two glasses of water, one after another, that are at different temperatures, you can tell which one is warmer—even if the difference is only a few degrees.

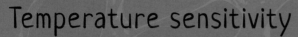

TRY IT YOURSELF

1. Ask an adult to help you get two cups of warm water (not too hot—you don't want to burn yourself). Add a little cold water to one cup.

2. Dip your right index finger into the warmer water, and your left index finger into the cooler one.

3. After 30 seconds, switch your fingers to the other cups. You should be able to feel the left finger getting warmer while the right one gets cooler.

Touch

When you want to gather information on an object, you probably look at it first. But after you've looked at it you might touch it, feel it, or pick it up. We get a lot of information about the world around us through our sense of touch. Some areas of our skin are more sensitive than others.

TRY IT YOURSELF

1. Open a paperclip and bend it into a U-shape with the two ends slightly apart.

2. Press the points gently against the skin on a fingertip. Can you feel one point or two?

3. Try this on different parts of the body. In some places you will feel two separate points, but in others you will only feel one. This is because some areas have more touch receptors than others.

Control of body temperature

The parts of your skin that help control your body's temperature are the hairs, the sweat **glands**, and the **capillaries**. If you are cold, the hairs on your body stand on end. Each hair has its own tiny muscle to pull it upright. When the hair does this, it traps a layer of warm air next to the skin. In humans this isn't terribly effective, because we're not very hairy, but in other mammals and

birds it's very important. This is why small birds and mammals often look "fluffed up" in cold weather.

8

When you are cold, blood is redirected from the capillaries, near the surface of your skin, down to blood vessels deeper under the skin. This way, blood doesn't lose heat. When you are hot, the blood is sent to the skin capillaries in order to lose heat. The image below shows a cross-section of skin.

The sweat glands in your ears are modified to produce earwax instead of sweat!

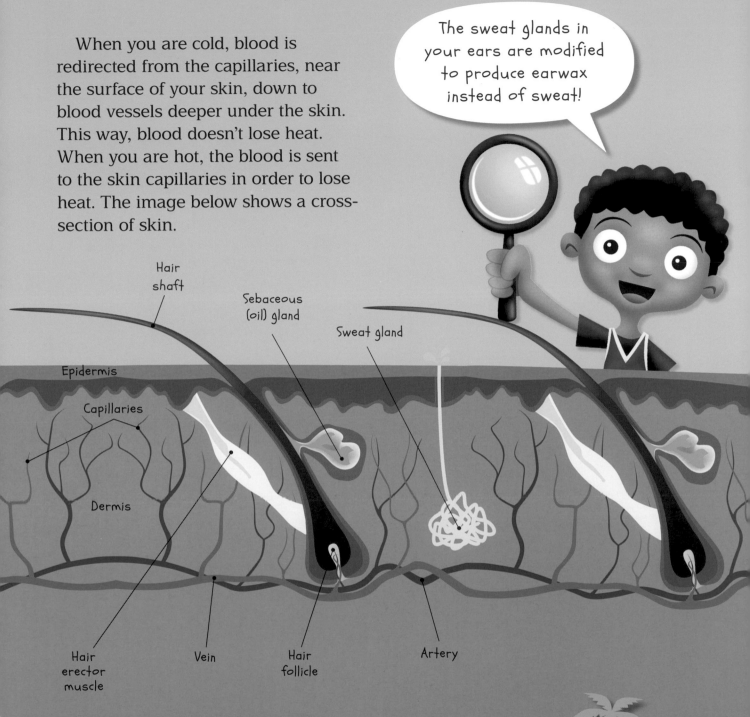

Hair shaft

Sebaceous (oil) gland

Sweat gland

Epidermis

Capillaries

Dermis

Hair erector muscle

Vein

Hair follicle

Artery

Your sweat glands produce sweat when you are hot, which is released onto the surface of the skin. In places with dry air, the sweat easily evaporates and cools the skin.

In places with **humid** air, such as in the tropics, the sweat doesn't evaporate as easily. This makes it harder to keep cool.

The Heart

Blood is moved around the entire body by the heart. Your heart acts as a pump in order to do this.

In fact, your heart is really two pumps stuck together side by side. The right side fills with blood from the body and sends it to the lungs to collect oxygen. At the same time, the left side fills with the blood from the lungs and sends it to the rest of the body.

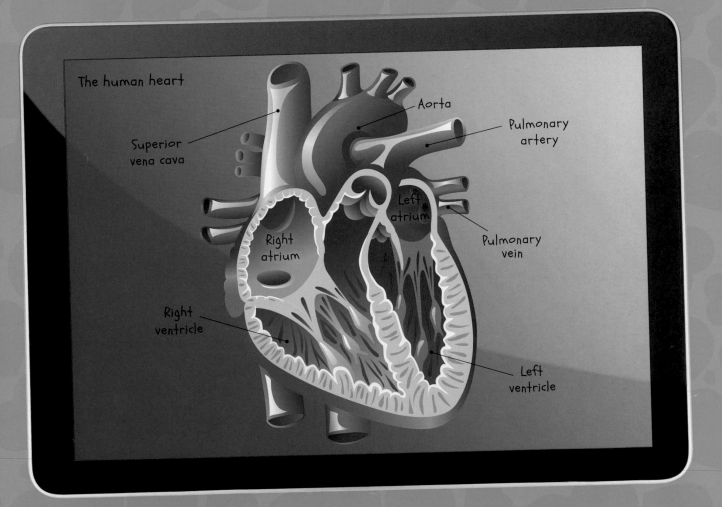

The human heart

Superior vena cava

Aorta

Pulmonary artery

Left atrium

Right atrium

Pulmonary vein

Right ventricle

Left ventricle

Pulse

It's usually quite hard to feel your heart beating, as it's hidden behind your ribs. However, you can feel the squirt of blood pushed out by each heartbeat, which is called the pulse. This happens in places where an artery is near the skin.

A pulse rate is the number of times per minute your heart pumps blood. It varies a lot from person to person, but the average is about 70 beats per minute.

Your pulse rate varies depending on what you are doing. Take it for a minute when you are sitting doing nothing and make a note of it. Now, if you are able, do some exercise until you are breathing heavily. You could run around your yard, jump up and down, skip, or chase your dog.

As soon as you stop, take your pulse again. It will be faster than before. This is because your muscles need more blood brought to them when you make them work. Take your pulse again five minutes after you have stopped exercising. It should be more or less back to normal.

TRY IT YOURSELF

The easiest place to find your pulse is on your wrist or neck. Use your fingers to take your pulse. Don't use your thumb because it has a pulse, too. Using your thumb can make it difficult to find your correct pulse rate.

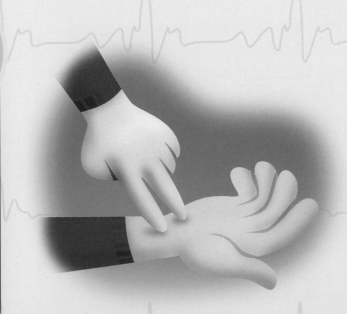

Taking your pulse

The Blood System

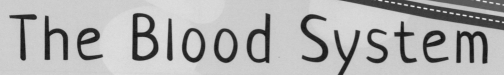

The blood system is the transportation system of the body. Blood vessels are like different types of roads. The largest **arteries** and **veins** are like highways. Branching off from them are smaller vessels which are like main city roads. The smallest vessels, known as capillaries, are like side roads. Substances in the blood, such as oxygen and **glucose** sugar, move from the capillaries to other body cells.

Your biggest artery is called the **aorta**. It is about the same diameter as your thumb. It carries blood out of the left ventricle of the heart and sends it on its journey around the body. Other arteries branch off the aorta at various points, taking supplies of **nutrients** and oxygen to different organs and muscles.

What happens if you don't let blood bring supplies of nutrients and oxygen to your muscles when they're working? Try the activity on page 13 and find out!

> All carbon dioxide is taken from the vital organs to the lungs, where it is breathed out!

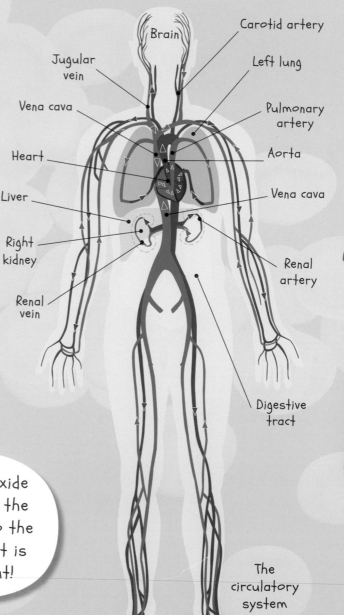

Brain
Carotid artery
Jugular vein
Left lung
Vena cava
Pulmonary artery
Heart
Aorta
Liver
Vena cava
Right kidney
Renal artery
Renal vein
Digestive tract

The circulatory system

Try it yourself

- Put one arm straight up in the air and let your other arm hang down by your side. Now clench and unclench both fists as hard as you can, about once every second.

- The hand that's up in the air will begin to hurt and your fingers will feel stiff.

- Stop clenching now and put down the arm that was in the air. In fact, if you don't, your muscles will do it for you because they'll get a **cramp**.

- So what just happened? Your muscles need oxygen and glucose sugar, which are carried by your blood, so that they can **contract**. They contract when you clench and unclench your hands.

- It's easy for blood to get to the muscles of the hand that's hanging down. But, it's much harder for blood to get to the hand that's up in the air because it has to flow against the pull of gravity.

- When your muscles don't get enough oxygen, a **toxic** substance called lactic acid builds up in them. This makes your muscles feel stiff and then cramp.

- When you put your arm down again blood can carry the lactic acid away to be broken down and the cramp stops.

Valves

One place where blood has to flow against gravity is from your feet and up your legs so it can get back to your heart. To help it along, the veins in your legs have valves in them to keep blood flowing in the right direction.

Blood can flow more easily from your legs to your heart when you stand on your hands.

Why don't my ankles fill up with blood?

Closed Valves   Opened Valves

 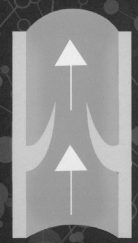

Valves close to stop blood from flowing in the wrong direction, such as back down the leg.

Valves open to help the blood continue its flow in the right direction.

TRY IT YOURSELF

• If you clench your fist, you should see a pattern of bluish veins appear just under the skin on the back of your hand.

• With your finger, press down hard on an vein near your wrist, and stroke it toward your knuckles. The blue color should disappear from a section of the vein.

• When you take your finger away you should see it refill from the knuckle end. (This works best if your hands are warm.)

• What has happened is that you have massaged the blood out of a section of vein. By pressing on it, you've prevented it from refilling from the knuckle

end of the vein. The one-way valves prevent it from refilling from the wrist end.

• Make sure you wait a few minutes before trying this again.

Hand veins

All veins have valves in them. In your hands, the veins are just under your skin, and you can see how the valves work.

15

The Digestive System

I bet you've never thought of yourself as a donut. Well, in a way, you are like one. Like a donut, you've got a hole that runs all the way through the middle of you, but it's much longer and wigglier than a donut hole.

This wobbly hole is your digestive system, and it goes all the way from your mouth at the top of your body, to your anus at the bottom—a distance of about 33 feet (10 meters).

Before the food you eat can do any good, it has to get out of your digestive system and into the rest of your body. In order for this to happen, two key things need to take place—digestion and absorption.

The digestive system

Mouth

Esophagus

Gall Bladder

Liver

Stomach

Pancreas

Duodenum

Small intestine

Large intestine

Appendix

Rectum

Anus

Digestion is breaking food down into small molecules. **Absorption** is moving these molecules through the wall of the digestive system and into the blood.

Digestion in the mouth

The digestion of food starts in your mouth.

TRY IT YOURSELF

• Get a soda cracker and make sure it doesn't have any sugar in it. Break it up into pieces, put it into your mouth and start chewing.

• Keep chewing!

• You need to keep the cracker in your mouth for about two minutes. It's quite hard not to swallow it, but try to resist!

• As time goes on, the mushy cracker should start to taste sweet. This is because a chemical in your saliva has broken down the big molecules of **starch** in the cracker into small molecules of sugar—which of course tastes sweet.

• You can swallow now, and you'll probably want a drink of water to wash all the mushy cracker off your teeth!

17

Digestion in the stomach

To be further digested, food moves from your mouth to your stomach, which is a muscular bag. When it's empty, it has a volume of about 1.7–2.4 fluid ounces (50–70 milliliters). Normally, it can stretch to hold about 34 fluid ounces (1 liter). If forced, it can stretch to hold about 68–101 fluid ounces (2–3 L), but that's very uncomfortable. Your stomach makes hydrochloric acid, which kills **microbes** on your food and helps break down protein.

No wonder it makes such funny noises!

Digestion in the small intestine

Food moves from your stomach into your small intestine for complete digestion. Here, the food is broken down into molecules small enough to flow from the digestive system into the blood and travel to the rest of the body. Nutrients from the food molecules are **absorbed** into the blood through millions of tiny projections called villi, which stick out into the small intestine. Even though each villus is only about 0.07–0.1 inches (2–3 mm) long, altogether they provide a huge surface area—about the size of a tennis court!

Imagine this is the size of your small intestine!

By the time food gets to the end of the small intestine, all the useable nutrients have been absorbed. What is left is mainly fiber, or tiny pieces of plant cells we can't digest, and water. Much of the water is removed in the large intestine, so by the time the waste gets to the end of the digestive system at the rectum and anus, it is semi-solid.

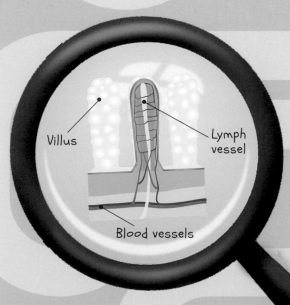

Villus

Lymph vessel

Blood vessels

Close up of villi

The correct scientific name for the semi-solid waste is feces, but you probably know it by other names!

The Lungs

The job of your lungs is to move air in and out of your body. Oxygen from inhaled air passes from your lungs into your blood. Your blood then carries the oxygen to all your cells. Blood also carries the carbon dioxide produced in your cells back to your lungs. Your lungs get rid the carbon dioxide when you exhale. Breathing out is just as important as breathing in!

You breathe out to blow up a balloon or to blow bubbles.

Air breathed in:
79% nitrogen
20% oxygen
0.03% carbon dioxide

Air breathed out:
79% nitrogen
16% oxygen
3% carbon dioxide

The air you breathe in is made up of approximately 79% nitrogen, 20% oxygen, and 0.03% carbon dioxide. You probably think that all of the oxygen is absorbed when it's in your lungs, but it's not. The air you breathe out is approximately 79% nitrogen, 16% oxygen, and 3% carbon dioxide.

Exhaled air

Breathing out oxygen makes sense if you think about it—**mouth-to-mouth resuscitation** couldn't work unless there was a fairly high oxygen content in exhaled air. The carbon dioxide has increased in the air you breathe out because it's a waste product of chemical reactions in your cells.

Carbon dioxide is toxic, so you have to get rid of it quickly. In fact, your body is more sensitive to changes in carbon dioxide levels than it is to changes in oxygen levels. When you hold your breath, it's the increased carbon dioxide that makes you breathe again, not the fact that your body is running out of oxygen.

The respiratory system

Nasal cavity

Trachea

Bronchi

Inhaling and Exhaling

Lungs

Diaphragm

Turn to the next page to find out what is inside your lungs!

21

Pleural membrane

Bronchi

Bronchioles

Alveoli

The human lungs

Holding your breath

The average person can hold their breath for 30–40 seconds, but if you look up world records, you'll find people who can hold their breath for several minutes! Most of these records are set under cold water. This is because oxygen **consumption** and carbon dioxide production slow down when the body is in cold water, allowing a person to hold their breath for longer periods of time. This can be very dangerous, so do not try this yourself!

What are your lungs like inside?

You might think that your lungs are like balloons, but in fact they are more like sponges. Instead of a large, open space inside them, there are millions of tiny spaces. These tiny air sacs are called **alveoli**. Alveoli are surrounded by blood vessels called capillaries. Oxygen travels from the alveoli into the capillaries, and then throughout your body in your blood. Carbon dioxide leaves your body in a similar way. It moves through your body in your blood until it gets to the capillaries. It then passes through into the alveoli, and is breathed out each time you exhale.

Capillaries

Alveoli

Bronchioles close-up

TRY IT YOURSELF

How much do your lungs hold? Ask an adult to help you with the following experiment.

You will need:

1 measuring cup

1 empty plastic bottle—about 0.5–1 gallon (2–3 liters)

A waterproof marker

1 piece of clean flexible plastic tubing (you can get this from aquarium supply stores, or maybe your school science department might lend you a piece)

1. Use the measuring cup to put 2 cups (500 ml) of water into the bottle.

2. Mark the water level on the side of the bottle with the marker.

3. Add another 2 cups (500 ml) and mark the new level.

4. Keep doing this until the bottle is full.

5. Put about 1 inch (2–3 cm) of water in a sink or bucket.

6. Put your hand over the top of the full bottle, turn it upside down, put the top of the bottle under the water in the sink or bucket and take your hand away. All the water should stay in the bottle!

7. Carefully, wiggle one end of the plastic tubing inside the bottle top.

8. Take a deep breath, put the other end of the tube in your mouth, and blow as hard as you can! Make sure you don't accidentallybreathe in and swallow the water!

9. The air you blow out pushes the same amount of water out of the bottle. You can use the measurements you put on the bottle to find out how much air you were able to breathe out.

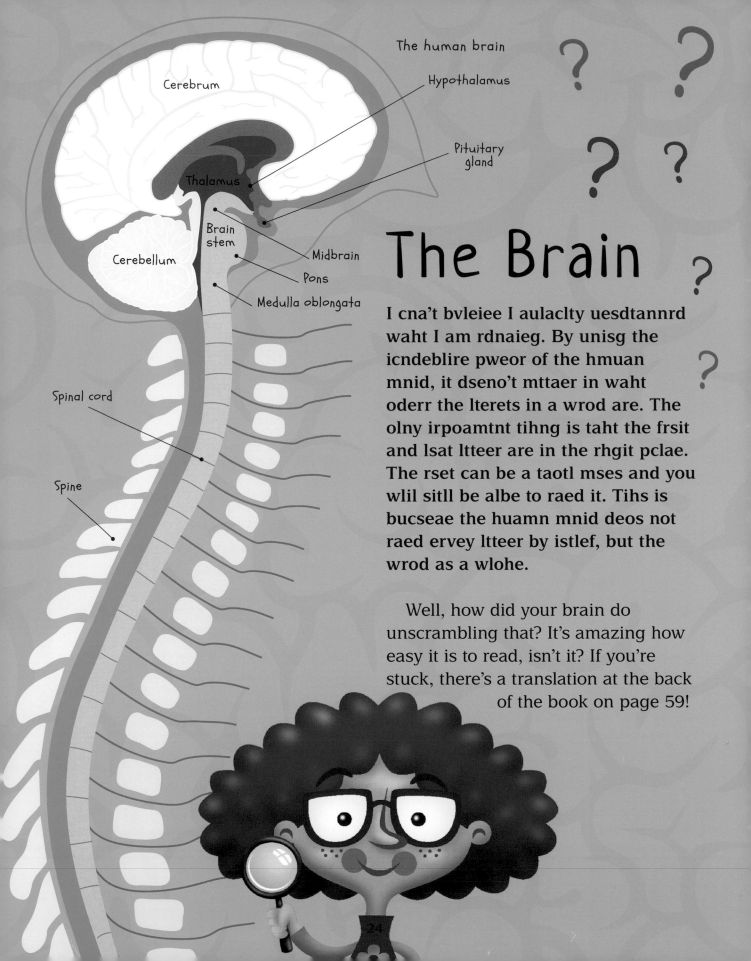

The human brain

Cerebrum

Hypothalamus

Pituitary gland

Thalamus

Brain stem

Cerebellum

Midbrain

Pons

Medulla oblongata

Spinal cord

Spine

The Brain

I cna't bvleiee I aulaclty uesdtannrd waht I am rdnaieg. By unisg the icndeblire pweor of the hmuan mnid, it dseno't mttaer in waht oderr the lterets in a wrod are. The olny irpoamtnt tihng is taht the frsit and lsat ltteer are in the rhgit pclae. The rset can be a taotl mses and you wlil sitll be albe to raed it. Tihs is bucseae the huamn mnid deos not raed ervey ltteer by istlef, but the wrod as a wlohe.

Well, how did your brain do unscrambling that? It's amazing how easy it is to read, isn't it? If you're stuck, there's a translation at the back of the book on page 59!

• The brain contains between 85 billion and 100 billion cells.

• The brain and spinal cord are kind of like a long, wrinkled sock. The "foot" of the sock is folded back to make the brain. The "leg" of the sock is the spinal cord, which runs down the inside of the backbone. The brain and spinal cord are hollow, just like the sock, but unlike the sock (unless you're washing it) they are filled with and surrounded by fluid.

• Human brains are three times bigger than other mammals their size.

Bizarre brain facts

Of all the extraordinary organs of the body, the brain is the most amazing. Here are a few mind-boggling statistics.

• Each cell is connected to about 10,000 other brain cells.

• The brain has no pain receptors, so it cannot feel pain.

• The brain makes up only about 2% of our bodyweight, but uses about 20% of the body's energy.

• The brain is protected by your skull, which is made of 22 bones.

• The right side of your brain controls the left side of your body, and the left side of your brain controls the right side of your body!

• Your brain stops producing new cells when you are about 18. When the cells die, they usually aren't replaced.

Brain functions

Below is a diagram of the human brain and its various functions.

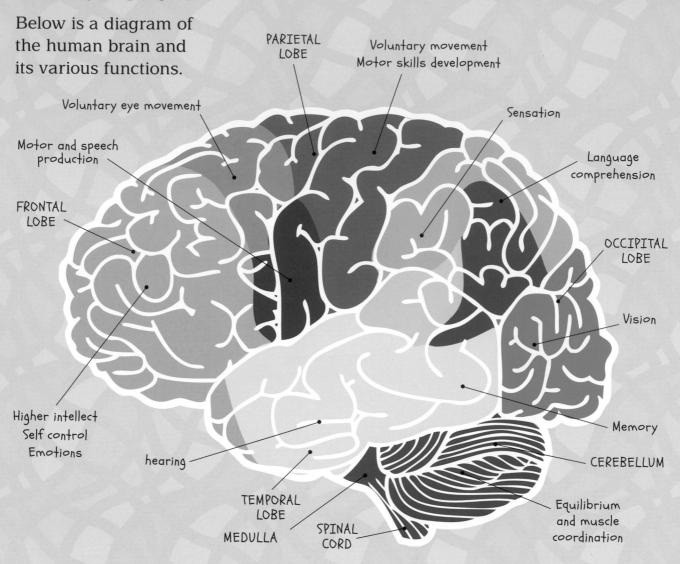

PARIETAL LOBE

Voluntary movement
Motor skills development

Voluntary eye movement

Sensation

Motor and speech production

Language comprehension

FRONTAL LOBE

OCCIPITAL LOBE

Vision

Higher intellect
Self control
Emotions

Memory

hearing

CEREBELLUM

TEMPORAL LOBE

Equilibrium and muscle coordination

MEDULLA

SPINAL CORD

Cerebral hemispheres

Different areas of the brain have different jobs. All the things that make you "you" happen in the **cerebral hemispheres**. This is where signals from your sense organs are processed, and where the nerve impulses to your muscles start. It's also the area responsible for speech, personality, and memory.

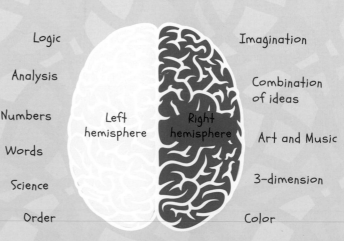

Logic

Imagination

Analysis

Combination of ideas

Numbers

Left hemisphere

Right hemisphere

Art and Music

Words

Science

3-dimension

Order

Color

The jobs of each hemisphere of our brain.

26

Cerebellum

The **cerebellum** is where complicated movements are controlled. When you learn to do something like ride a bike or play a musical instrument, it's your cerebellum that "learns" the sequence of movements. Once you have learned something, the information can be stored for years. For example, riding a bike is a skill you will remember how to do, even if you don't get on a bicycle for years.

Optical illusions

The jumbled passage on page 24 shows how efficient the brain is at sorting out mixed up things, but you can fool it.

This is how **optical illusions** work. The brain uses information from the eyes and tries to make sense of what it's seeing. Optical illusions use colors, light, and patterns to trick the brain into seeing something that may not be real.

Medulla

The **medulla** keeps you breathing and keeps your heart beating. These are automatic functions, so you don't have to remember to do them. Imagine how difficult it would be if you were eating your lunch and having a conversation, and you had to decide when to take each breath so you could keep doing both!

Do I breathe or do I eat?

The Nervous System

The nervous system brings information to your brain and spinal cord, and carries signals from them telling the rest of your body what to do. The fastest signals are called **reflexes**. These are very fast reactions that happen in potentially damaging situations. Fast reflexes help to prevent the damage from taking place. To make them as fast as possible, reflexes don't even involve the brain. Information goes to the spinal cord and straight back out again.

For instance, if you accidentally put your finger on a hot surface, you pull it away so quickly that it doesn't hurt until after your finger is removed. This is because pain sensors in your skin send a signal to your spinal cord, which sends another signal straight to the muscles of the hand and arm telling them to get that finger off of there! Meanwhile, another signal goes to the brain, but it takes longer, because it has further to travel. This is the one that lets you know it hurts, but you've already removed your finger from danger. Definitely don't try this yourself!

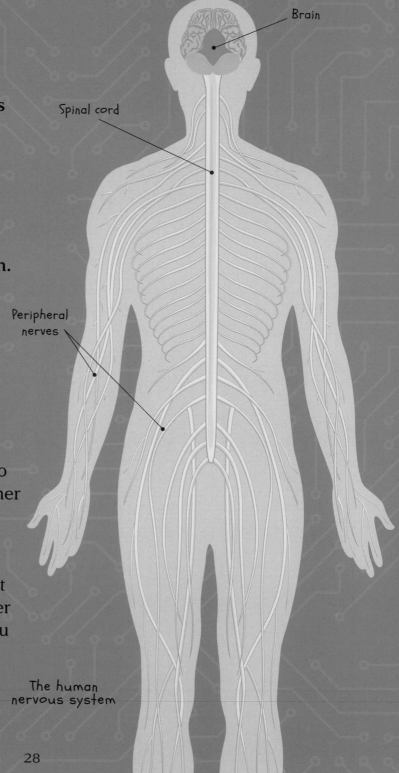

Brain

Spinal cord

Peripheral nerves

The human nervous system

Reflexes

▶You have a lot of reflexes: coughing, sneezing, knee-jerk, blinking, and many more.

TRY IT YOURSELF

Here are two reflexes you can investigate safely. Turn to page 30 for the second experiment.

1. You can find the knee-jerk reflex quite easily.

• Get a partner to sit with their legs crossed, so that their top leg swings freely and their foot doesn't touch the ground.

• Use your hand to feel for the lower edge of their knee cap, just below the knee.

• Use the side of your hand furthest from your thumb to hit just below the knee cap, but not too hard!

• If you hit the right place, the lower leg will immediately kick out. Make sure you're not standing in the way when it does!

Try it yourself

2. The pupil of your eye is the black part in the middle of the iris, or colored part. It regulates how much light gets in and reaches the **retina** at the back of the eye. In bright light, the pupil is quite small, because too much light can damage the retina. In dim light, however, it gets much bigger to let in more light. This helps you see more. There are two ways you can investigate this.

• In a brightly lit room, get a friend to close their eyes tightly and put their hands over their eyes to make it extra dark. Have them stay like this for 30 seconds. When they open their eyes again, watch closely and you will see their pupils shrink—it happens quickly, so be ready!

• You can do this experiment by yourself, too. Sit in front of a mirror in a brightly lit room. Shut and cover one eye as described earlier. Watch your eyes in the mirror as you open the closed eye. You should see that the pupil of the closed eye is bigger than the one that was open, but quickly shrinks to the same size.

Pupils in bright light

Pupils in dim light

Reaction time

Reaction time is the time between seeing or hearing a signal, and starting to move in response to it. For most people, reaction time is about 0.25 seconds, but for top athletes, especially **sprinters**, it is faster—between 0.12 and 0.18 seconds. This can make a big difference as to who wins a race.

There is a limit to how fast you can react. It takes a certain minimum time for you to hear or see the start signal, for your brain to process that information, and for it to send a message to your muscles to start moving. The shortest time this can take is 0.11 seconds.

If the athlete starts to move less than 0.11 seconds after the starting signal, their brain must have sent the signal to their muscles before the start signal. Therefore, even though they didn't move until after the signal, it's still a false start, and the runner is penalized.

TRY IT YOURSELF

You can test your own reaction time with a 12-inch (30-centimeter) ruler—but you also need a friend to help you.

1. Get your friend to hold the ruler with the 0 mark down.

2. Place your thumb and forefinger on either side of the 0 inch (cm) mark, but don't touch the ruler.

3. Ask your friend to let go of the ruler and see how fast you can catch it. Make a note of how many inches (cm) it falls.

4. Do this ten times. Add up your results and divide by ten to get your average. There is a chart on page 58 that lets you convert your average into a reaction time.

The Nose and Tongue

Your senses of smell and taste are very hard to separate. Often what we think is a food's taste is actually its smell. You might be aware of this when you have a cold—if your nose is plugged, food seems to lose a lot of its taste.

Smell

Your nose is lined with special **receptor cells** which can detect about 1,000 different types of chemicals. Each chemical fits into a special area on the surface of one type of cell, like a key fitting into a lock. When this happens, a signal is sent to the brain. The brain interprets this signal as a smell.

We have about 1,000 different types of receptor cells, but scientists think we can identify up to 10,000 different smells. This works the same way that the 26 letters of the alphabet can be used to make thousands of different words—by combining signals from different receptor cells when they get to the brain.

Some people have a much more sensitive sense of smell than others, and your sense of smell gets poorer as you get older. If you have a really good sense of smell, you could end up working as a "nose," or perfumer. This is someone who develops perfumes.

Here's a puzzle: no one really understands how we can remember smells. The cells in your nose die and are replaced all the time, but you don't forget what oranges or roses smell like.

One of the most expensive perfume scents is called Ambergris. It is produced in the digestive system of a whale!

Perfume Recipe

TOP SECRET

TRY IT YOURSELF

Think about what you're smelling! Although we are very sensitive to smells, we often don't pay much attention to them (unless they're really delicious or really horrible). What does a tennis ball smell like? Or a leaf? Or this book?

Blindfold a friend and let them smell a lot of different things (nothing too horrible though—you still want them to be your friend when you finish the experiment!).

Try using fruits, herbs, and spices from the kitchen; soaps and lotions from the bathroom; and, of course, perfume. How many can they identify?

Taste

Look at your tongue in the mirror. It's covered in little bumps. It's OK, it's supposed to look like that! Those bumps are your taste buds. They contain receptor cells, similar to the ones in your nose, but they can't detect nearly as many different chemicals.

TRY IT YOURSELF

Make a taste map of your tongue! You will need:

1/4 cup (60 ml) of water with about 1/4 teaspoon (1 ml) of salt in it (salty)

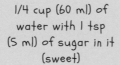

1/4 cup (60 ml) of water with 1 tsp (5 ml) of sugar in it (sweet)

The juice of half a lemon (sour)

Tonic water (bitter)

Soy sauce (umami)

Cotton swabs

1. Draw a large tongue shape on a sheet of paper.

2. Dip a cotton swab in the salty water. Dab it onto different areas of your tongue. Make a note on your tongue diagram of where you can taste salt.

3. Using a fresh cotton swab, repeat with each of the other liquids.

4. Now you should have a map of which parts of your tongue are sensitive to which flavors. Check the one on page 35 to see if you agree.

There are only five different basic tastes. They are sweet, salty, sour, bitter, and **umami**. (Umami is a Japanese word for a really savory flavor, and it has only recently been discovered that it's a basic taste.)

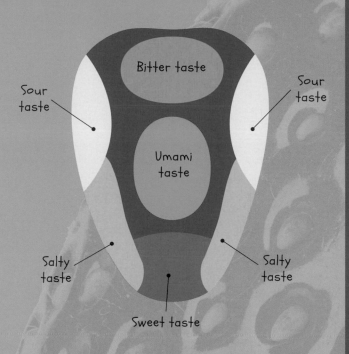

Bitter taste

Sour taste

Sour taste

Umami taste

Salty taste

Salty taste

Sweet taste

Tongue taste map

Fooling your sense of taste

What you think of as your sense of taste is partly your sense of smell, but that's not all. Your sense of taste is also influenced by what your food looks like…

TRY IT YOURSELF

Ask an adult if you can carry out the following experiments to see how your senses of smell and sight affect your taste.

1. Ask an adult to help you cut some small cubes of peeled apple, onion, and carrot.

2. Blindfold a friend and get them to hold their nose tightly—make sure they remember to breathe through their mouth!

3. Have your blindfolded friend stick their tongue out, and put a cube of food on it. See if your friend can identify it using only taste, without smell to help them. It's not as easy as you think!

To see how the color of food affects your sense of taste, you need to make some jelly. You will need:

• Gelatin or the vegetarian equivalent

• Food coloring

• Flavorings

Make up the jelly according to the instructions on the gelatin packet, add flavoring, but then add the wrong color. For instance, you could make strawberry-flavored jelly and then add green food coloring, or pink lemon jelly, or blue apple jelly! When it's set, see if other people can determine what the flavor is. Make up a few different combinations and have fun!

The Ears

Your ears allow you to hear, but they also help to prevent you from falling over. No, not because they're really big or stick out, but because they are responsible for your sense of balance.

Hearing

Humans don't have particularly good hearing. If you have a dog, you'll know that they can hear sounds that are much quieter and higher-pitched than us. You may also have noticed that, unlike humans, they can move their ears to help them detect sound.

Here's how your ears work to let you hear sounds. Sound waves hit the eardrum and make it vibrate. These vibrations are passed on to the hammer, anvil, and stirrup (the three smallest bones in the body). As these bones vibrate, they amplify sounds by about 20 times. So what you're hearing is really 20 times quieter than it sounds! The vibrations are passed on through other parts of the ear until they reach the cochlea. Here, special cells change them into electrical signals, which travel along the **auditory** nerve to the brain.

Animals such as dolphins and bats use **ultrasound** to communicate. These are high-pitched sounds above the human hearing range, so most people cannot hear them. Elephants and giraffes communicate using infrasounds. These are low-pitched sounds under the human hearing range, so we cannot hear them very well.

Below is a diagram of the human ear.

Anvil

Inner ear

Hammer

Stirrup

Ear canal

Cochlea

Outer ear

Eardrum

Middle ear

Age and hearing

As you get older, you become less able to hear very high-pitched sounds. Children can hear the ultrasonic sounds that bats make, but adults can't. There's a rather sneaky piece of modern technology called the Mosquito Anti-Loitering Device that makes use of this fact. It is used to stop children and teenagers from hanging around places they shouldn't be. It makes a high-pitched buzz, which can only be heard if you are a child or teenager.

Balance

In the inner ear, buried deep inside your skull, are liquid-filled tubes that give you your sense of balance. They send messages about the position of your head to your brain. This will often save you from falling if you trip or lose your balance—your brain gets information that the position of your head has changed in an unexpected way and is able to make corrections fast enough for you to stay on your feet.

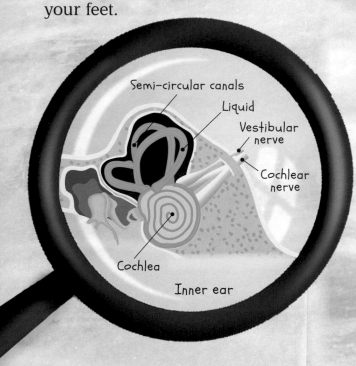

Semi-circular canals

Liquid

Vestibular nerve

Cochlear nerve

Cochlea

Inner ear

It's also the balance apparatus in your ears that makes you dizzy if you spin around and around. In your inner ear, there are three semi-circular tubes, or canals, at right angles to each other. They are filled with liquid.

You can stir a glass of water to get a better idea of how these work. While you're stirring, the water goes around and around, and it keeps going around and around for a while even after you stop stirring.

This is what happens to the liquid in the semi-circular canals if you spin around and around. It starts moving as you spin, but when you stop, it keeps going. This means your ears are telling your brain that you're still moving, but your eyes are telling your brain that you have stopped. No wonder your brain gets confused!

Ice skaters and ballet dancers are people that have to do a lot of spinning without getting dizzy and falling over. Do they have ears that are different from other people? No! They have a special trick called "spotting" to avoid getting dizzy.

TRY IT YOURSELF

Try this special spotting trick yourself! You're going to be spinning around, so make sure you do it somewhere safe so that if you fall over you won't hurt yourself or break anything. Before starting this experiment, ask an adult to make sure it's ok.

You already know that if you just spin around and around you'll get dizzy, so you don't need to try that. Instead, here's how to avoid getting dizzy.

- Look at something that is about eye level. Maybe a picture on the wall, or a clock if you're indoors, or a tree or a door if you are outside.

- Slowly turn your body, keeping your head still for as long as possible and still staring at the same spot.

- When you feel you can't turn your body any further without moving your head, turn your head around quickly and stare at the same spot again.

- Once you get the hang of it, try the same technique when you spin around quickly. If you do this each time you spin, you don't get dizzy. This is because your head only moves for a very short time, and the liquid in your semi-circular canals doesn't have enough time to start moving.

- If at any point you do start to feel dizzy, make sure you stop and sit down until you feel ok again.

The Eye

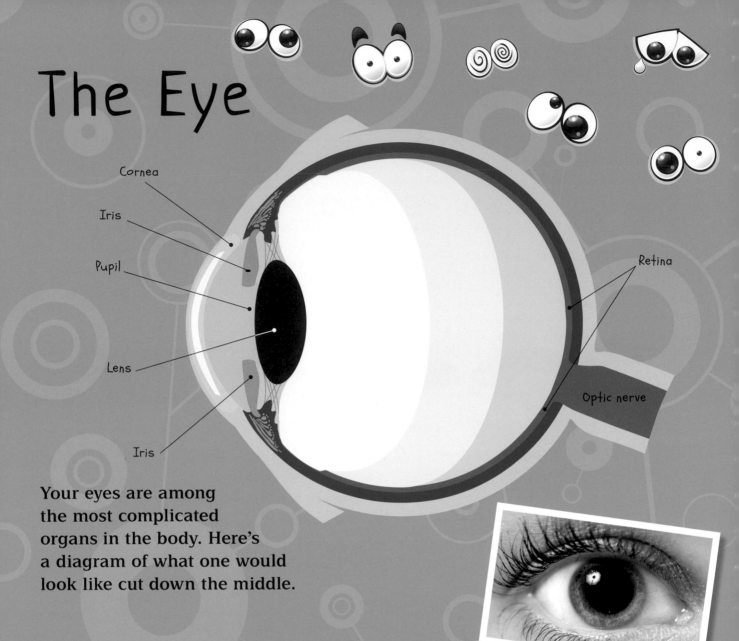

Cornea

Iris

Pupil

Lens

Iris

Retina

Optic nerve

Your eyes are among the most complicated organs in the body. Here's a diagram of what one would look like cut down the middle.

Dilated pupil

Letting light into the eye

The pupil and iris control how much light gets into the eye. The pupil is a hole in the center of the iris, or the colored part of your eye. The iris is a ring of muscle that can contract and **relax** to change the size of the pupil in the middle. In bright light, your pupils are quite small, but in dim light they get wider so as much

light as possible can get into the eyes. If you go from bright light into a dark room, you can't see much at first. Your eyes gradually become "dark adapted" as the pupils dilate, or open wide. If you then go back into bright light you have to shield your eyes for a few seconds, because your wide pupils let in too much light.

Focusing

Your cornea and lens focus light so that a sharp image forms on the retina. If you are nearsighted or farsighted however, it's a blurry image, unless you wear glasses or contact lenses.

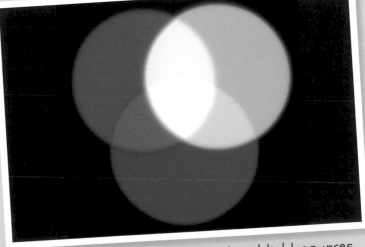

The way the human eye mixes colored light sources (red, blue, and green) to form a colored image

How the retina works

The retina is covered with cells that detect light. They are called rods and cones. There are three types of cones, which are sensitive to red, blue, and green light. These give you color vision. They also give you a really detailed picture. When you look at something, you are pointing the area of the retina with the most cones at it.

Rods only give you a picture in shades of gray, and in less detail than the cones. So, you might think they're not really useful—but they can work in much dimmer light than the cones. It's rods that let you see in dim light, or at night, and this is why you see everything in shades of gray at night.

41

TRY IT YOURSELF

On a clear, starry night, you can see the difference in how your rods and cones work. Look at a really dim star. Now look slightly to one side of it, and it will look brighter. This is because when you look straight at it you are pointing your cones at it, which are in the center of the retina, and they don't work very well in dim light. When you look to one side you see it more clearly, because you are pointing your rods at it, which are around the edge of the retina. They work properly even in dim light.

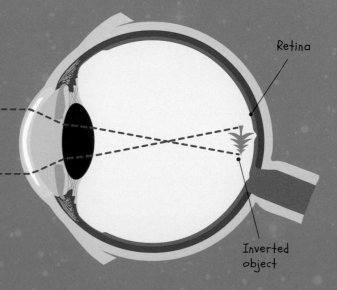

Seeing the right way up!

The image that forms on your retina is upside down! It's your brain that turns it the right way up again. If you give someone special goggles that turn things upside down, the image on the retina is the right way up, but your brain still reverses it, so you see things upside down. However, your brain will adjust to what is going on after a couple of days, and turn things the right way up again. Of course, once you take the glasses off, everything is upside down again for a while...

Retina

Object

Inverted object

TRY IT YOURSELF

You can demonstrate the upside down image by making a pinhole camera.

1. Take an empty potato chip tube.

2. Get an adult to cut all the way around the can about 2 inches (5 cm) from the metal end.

3. Get an adult to make a tiny hole in the center of the metal end using a thumb tack or push pin.

4. Place a circle of **tracing paper** inside the plastic lid—this will be the screen where you see the image.

5. Put the lid on the short piece of tube. Then attach the long piece of tube to the lid using masking tape.

6. Wrap a couple of layers of aluminum foil around the whole thing, leaving the ends open, and secure it with masking tape. This is to keep light out of the camera.

7. Take it outside on a sunny day and point the end with the pinhole at an object. Look through the open end. The object should appear upside down on the screen.

Why does this happen? It's because light travels in straight lines, so the light from the top of what you look at appears at the bottom of the screen.

(You can use a pinhole camera to take real photos if you are able to get some photographic film. See page 59 for a website address to learn how to do this.)

Pinhole camera

Photo taken using a pinhole camera

Blind spot

The light-sensitive cells on your retina are attached to nerve cells that carry messages to the brain. These messages all leave the retina at the same place, so there are no rods or cones on this part of the retina. This part is called the **blind spot**. You're not usually aware of its existence—there isn't a hole in the middle of what you see—but it's still there.

TRY IT YOURSELF

You can demonstrate the blind spot using the diagram below.

●   +

1. Hold the book up at arm's length so the dot and cross are at eye level.

2. Close your right eye and look at the cross with your left eye.

3. Keep looking at it and very slowly bring the book toward you.

4. At some point, the dot will disappear! This is because its image is falling on your blind spot.

5. Try it again. This time close your left eye and look at the dot with your right eye.

If we have blind spots, why don't we have holes in our vision? It's because our brain fills it in, taking its cues from what you see around that area. It's usually so successful that you don't notice, unless you trick your brain like in this experiment.

Why do you see stars if you hit your head?

If you've ever hit the back of your head, you know that you "see stars." Maybe not quite like cartoon characters do, with birds flying around your head tweeting while the stars twinkle, but definitely flashing starry lights. The reason for this is that although your eyes are at the front of your head, the part of your brain responsible for vision is at the back of your head. If you hit it, your brain gets all sorts of weird signals, which it interprets as flashing lights and stars.

Definitely do not try this yourself.

The Skeletal System

An adult human has 206 bones. The largest is the **femur**, or thigh bone, and you already know about the smallest ones—the ear ossicles, or tiny bones, known as the hammer, anvil, and stirrup (see page 37).

Bone is hard and strong (although it's not the hardest substance in the body—that's the **enamel** on your teeth) and mainly made of a mineral called **calcium** phosphate. It's the calcium that makes bones hard. If you could remove the calcium, the bone would become bendable! Get an adult to help you with the experiment below to make some bendable bones!

TRY IT YOURSELF

1. Get a leg or wing bone from a chicken. It doesn't matter if it's cooked or not.

2. Put the bone in a jar and cover it with vinegar.

3. Put the lid on the jar tightly, then wash your hands.

4. Leave it for at least three days.

5. After three days, take out the bone and rinse it under cold water.

6. The vinegar should have dissolved all the calcium in the bone, making the bone bendable. If it isn't bendable, put it back in the vinegar for another couple of days.

7. Wash your hands when you finish experimenting.

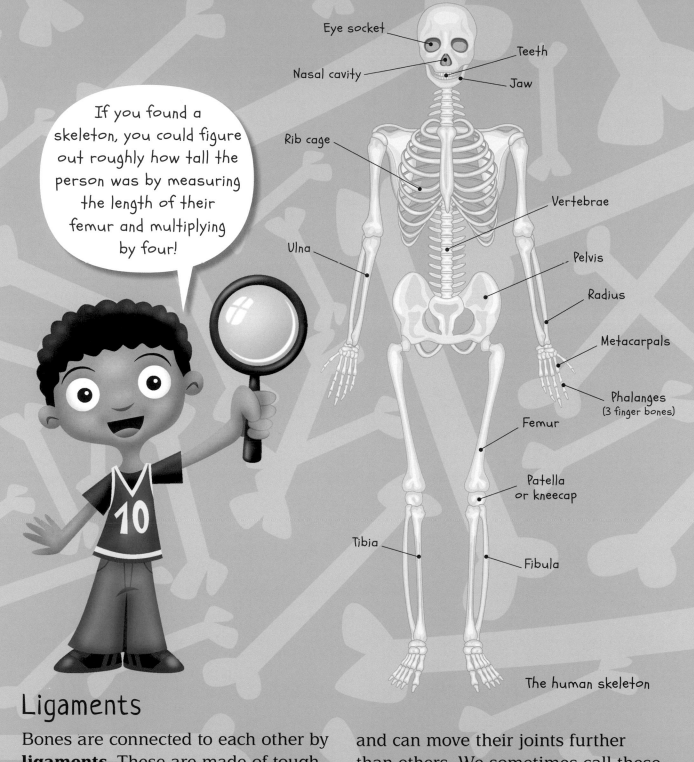

The human skeleton

Labels on the skeleton:
Eye socket · Teeth · Nasal cavity · Jaw · Rib cage · Vertebrae · Ulna · Pelvis · Radius · Metacarpals · Phalanges (3 finger bones) · Femur · Patella or kneecap · Tibia · Fibula

Speech bubble: If you found a skeleton, you could figure out roughly how tall the person was by measuring the length of their femur and multiplying by four!

Ligaments

Bones are connected to each other by **ligaments**. These are made of tough and slightly flexible tissue (not the kind you blow your nose with). Some people have extra-flexible ligaments and can move their joints further than others. We sometimes call these people "double-jointed," but they don't actually have twice as many joints.

The Muscle System

Muscles and bones work together to allow you to move. The bones form a system of levers, and the muscles pull on them.

All that spinach has made my muscles big and strong! But now none of my clothes fit!

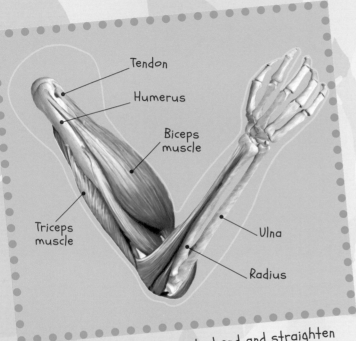

Tendon

Humerus

Biceps muscle

Triceps muscle

Ulna

Radius

Muscles that pull on bones to bend and straighten your arm

The biceps and triceps produce opposite effects when they contract. When the biceps contracts, the triceps relaxes and the arm bends at the elbow. When the triceps contracts the biceps relaxes and the arm straightens. If you bend your arm and tense your biceps you can see and feel it sticking up.

Muscles are connected to bones by **tendons**. It's important that tendons don't stretch because muscle contractions would stretch the tendon instead of pulling on the bone. Spinach is a great source of iron and vitamins that helps your muscles work better.

TRY IT YOURSELF

If you want to know more about muscles, tendons, bones, and ligaments, and how they fit together, try the experiment found on the website on page 59. Make sure you ask an adult's permission before you start your experiment, and get them to help you do the cutting.

For the experiment you will need:

A chicken wing

A small pair of sharp, pointed scissors and a small sharp knife

Some disposable gloves (but these aren't essential)

A magnifying glass

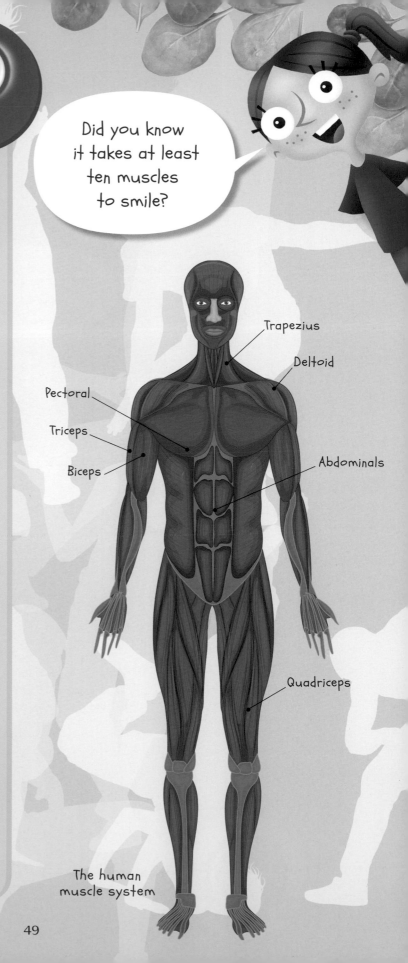

Did you know it takes at least ten muscles to smile?

Trapezius

Deltoid

Pectoral

Triceps

Biceps

Abdominals

Quadriceps

The human muscle system

You can't try it yourself!

There are some systems in the body that you can't investigate by doing experiments at home. This doesn't mean they aren't important though!

Here's a quick tour of them.

The urinary system

If you eat more protein than you need, it gets broken down by the liver, because you can't store it in your body. One of the products of this breakdown is a toxic substance called **urea**, which your body needs to get rid of before it builds up.

This is your kidneys' job. Each kidney contains over one million tiny filtering units used to clean the blood. Once filtered, urea and other wastes are sent to the bladder as urine. As well as removing urea, the kidneys also make sure the right concentrations of water and salts are in the blood so that blood cells can work properly.

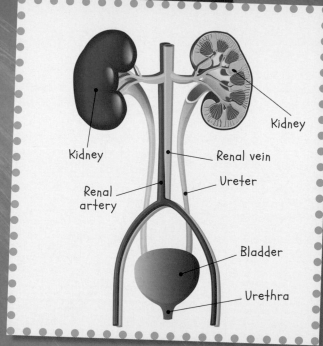

Urinary system

The kidneys are like a washing machine for your blood!

You have two kidneys, each about the size of the palm of your hand. Every minute, about 34 fluid ounces (1 L) of blood passes through them to be filtered and cleaned.

The reproductive system

The job of the reproductive system is to produce special cells called **gametes** (sperm in males and eggs in females) and make them meet. If they join together, the resulting fertilized egg can develop into a baby.

The female reproductive system

In females, the two ovaries release eggs at a rate of about one per month. Each egg is about the size of the period that the end of this sentence. Before birth, a baby girl's ovaries already contain all the eggs she will ever release. The uterus provides a place where a fertilized egg can develop into a baby.

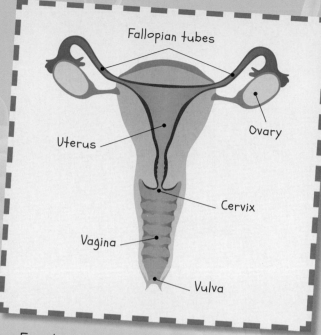

Female reproductive system

Fertilized egg

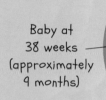

Baby at 38 weeks (approximately 9 months)

Elephants carry their babies for nearly two years!

51

Male reproductive system

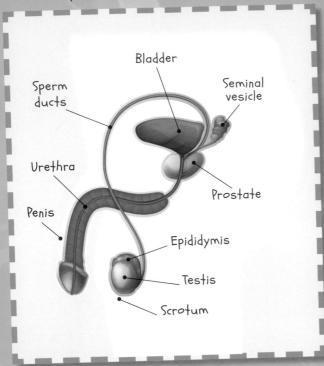

- Bladder
- Sperm ducts
- Seminal vesicle
- Urethra
- Prostate
- Penis
- Epididymis
- Testis
- Scrotum

Sperm swimming toward an egg

The male reproductive system

In adult males, the two testes produce sperm at the rate of 1000-1500 per second! Sperm are much smaller than eggs and, unlike eggs, they can swim (in fact, they look like tiny tadpoles). They are transferred into the female's reproductive system through the penis—then they have to swim. They all have to compete to get to the egg first. Only one can join with the egg to fertilize it. They only have about 7 inches (17.5 cm) to travel, but when you are only 0.001 inches (0.05 mm) long, that's a long way. It takes sperm anywhere from 45 minutes to three days to make the journey to the egg.

The lymphatic system

The lymphatic system is a sort of "shadow twin" to the blood system. Like the blood system, it has vessels that run all through the body. It also has swellings at various points, called **lymph** nodes. The lymphatic system has three different jobs:

1. It absorbs digested fats from the small intestine.

2. It mops up fluid that escapes from the blood capillaries and returns it to the blood system.

3. The lymph nodes contain many lymphocytes and act as a sort of security check on blood that passes through them. This is where antibodies and antigens get a chance to meet.

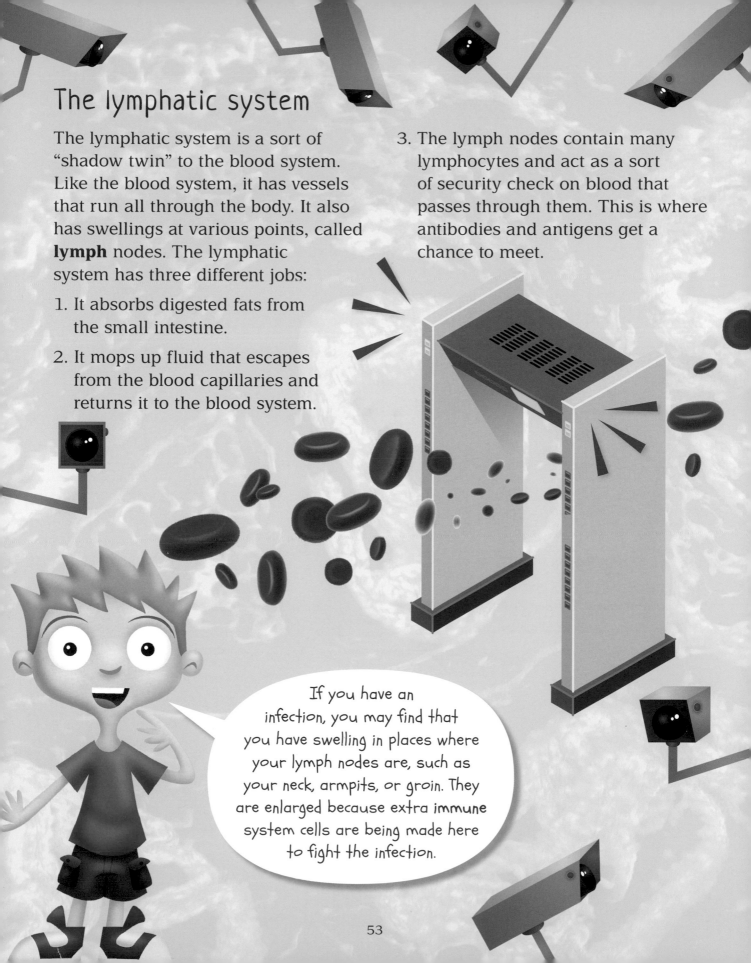

If you have an infection, you may find that you have swelling in places where your lymph nodes are, such as your neck, armpits, or groin. They are enlarged because extra immune system cells are being made here to fight the infection.

The hormone system

Hormones are chemicals that allow different parts of the body to communicate with each other. They are produced by glands in several areas of the body, and travel all around the body in the blood. Some hormones affect several organs. **Adrenalin**, which you make if you are scared, makes your heart beat faster, your pupils get wider, and your blood pressure increase. It diverts blood from the digestive system to the muscles, and suppresses your sense of pain and your need to urinate, or pee. All these things help prepare you for an emergency where you might have to fight or run away.

Scary or exciting activities, such as going on a roller coaster, make us produce adrenalin, too.

Other hormones only affect one organ. For instance, the antidiuretic hormone is produced in the brain, but only affects the tiny filtering units in the kidney. It makes sure they keep the right amount of water in the blood and send the rest out as urine.

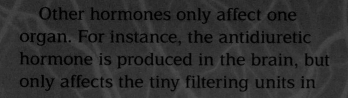

Girls produce some hormones in the ovaries, and boys produce the equivalent ones in the testes.

Male hormonal system

Pituitary gland

Thyroid gland

Thymus

Adrenal glands

Pancreas

Female hormonal system

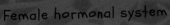

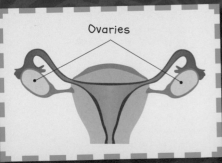

Ovaries

testes

The immune system

The immune system defends the body from foreign organisms such as bacteria and **viruses**. The two types of white blood cells in the immune system do this in different ways.

Below is how phagocytosis works...

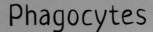

Phagocytes

One type of white blood cells, called **phagocytes**, creep up on foreign cells, gobble them up, and break them down. Although phagocytes are blood cells, they crawl out of the blood vessels and roam all over the body, looking for invading cells. If you have an infected cut or sore, you might see yellowish **pus** coming out of it. Pus is actually the bodies of brave phagocytes that have eaten themselves to death on bacteria as they defend you from disease.

1. Phagocyte meets bacterium.

Bacterium

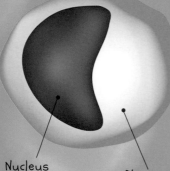

Nucleus

Phagocyte

2. Phagocyte engulfs bacterium.

3. Bacterium is destroyed by chemicals produced by phagocyte.

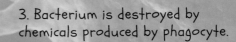

Bacterium broken down by chemicals

Lymphocytes

The other type of white blood cells are called lymphocytes. They stay in the blood and produce specially shaped proteins called antibodies. The antibodies fit perfectly onto molecules called antigens on the surface of foreign cells. The antibody and antigen fit together like a lock and key. The antibodies help destroy the foreign cells, but this can take a few days, so you might feel sick for a while before they are destroyed.

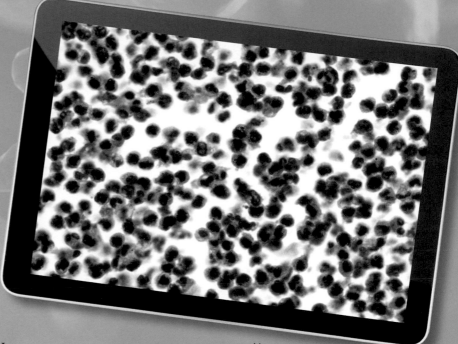

Human white blood cells

Antigen

Virus

Lymphocyte

Antibody

...and above is how antibodies defend you from intruders.

Some of the lymphocytes "remember" meeting certain viruses. If they come across them again, they produce antibodies so fast that you don't get sick. You become immune to these viruses, and won't catch them again.

Distance fallen	Reaction time (seconds)
0 in (0 cm)	0.00
0.4 in (1 cm)	0.04
0.8 in (2 cm)	0.06
1.2 in (3 cm)	0.08
1.6 in (4 cm)	0.09
2 in (5 cm)	0.10
2.4 in (6 cm)	0.11
2.8 in (7 cm)	0.12
3 in (8 cm)	0.13
3.5 in (9 cm)	0.14
4 in (10 cm)	0.14
4.3 in (11 cm)	0.15
4.7 in (12 cm)	0.16
5 in (13 cm)	0.16
5.5 in (14 cm)	0.17
6 in (15 cm)	0.18
6.3 in (16 cm)	0.18
6.7 in (17 cm)	0.19
7 in (18 cm)	0.19
7.5 in (19 cm)	0.20
7.9 in (20 cm)	0.20
8.3 in (21 cm)	0.21
8.7 in (22 cm)	0.21
9 in (23 cm)	0.21
9.4 in (24 cm)	0.22
9.8 in (25 cm)	0.23
10.2 in (26 cm)	0.23
10.6 in (27 cm)	0.23
11 in (28 cm)	0.24

Here is the chart to find out your reaction time in seconds, as mentioned on page 31.

Experiments

For the translation to the scrambled paragraph of text on page 24 see below:

I can't believe I can actually understand what I am reading. Using the incredible power of the human mind, it doesn't matter in what order the letters in a word are, the only important thing is that the first and last letter are in the right place. The rest can be a total mess and you can still read it without a problem. This is because the human mind does not read every letter by itself, but the word as a whole.

For more fun optical illusions like the ones on page 27, search Google images for "Magic Eye Illusions."

Visit this website for instructions on how to make a pinhole camera that will take a photograph (as mentioned on page 43).

www.matchboxpinhole.com/index.html

For instructions on how to **dissect** a chicken wing (as mentioned on page 49) visit the website below. Remember to ask an adult before you do this.

www.biologyalive.com/life/classes/ anatandphys/documents/Unit%206/ ChickenWingDissection.pdf

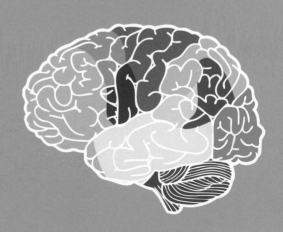

Find out more

Read

Slim Goodbody's Body Buddies series by John Burstein (Crabtree Publishing, 2009)

Human Body Mysteries Revealed by Natalie Hyde (Crabtree Publishing, 2010)

See for Yourself: Body Science by Catherine Chambers (Crabtree Publishing, 2011)

Watch

This interesting video from National Geographic gives more information on the human body and how it works:
http://video.nationalgeographic. com/video/101-videos/ human-body-sci

Find out more about how the digestive system works by watching this fun video:
http://kidshealth.org/kid/closet/ movies/DSmovie.html

Log on to

Learn more about how the body works at:
http://kidshealth.org/kid/htbw/

There are a lot of reaction time tests you can find on the Internet.
You can try one at:
www.mathsisfun.com/games/ reaction-time.html

Try and trick your brain with some of these fun optical illusions:
www.optics4kids.org/home/content/ illusions/

Find out more about how the digestive system works by watching this fun video:
http://kidshealth.org/kid/closet/ movies/DSmovie.html

Glossary

absorption Food molecules being moved through the wall of the digestive system into the blood

adrenalin A hormone that is produced by the body in stressful situations

alveoli Tiny air sacs in the lungs that help to move oxygen and carbon dioxide in and out of the blood

antibodies Proteins that fight off disease by helping to destroy bacteria or virus cells

antigens Molecules on the surface of foreign cells that cause the immune system to produce antibodies against them

aorta The biggest artery in the human body, carrying blood from the heart

arteries Blood vessels that carry blood containing oxygen and nutrients from the heart around the body

auditory Relating to the sense of hearing

blind spot The part of the retina that contains no rods or cones, so does not produce an image for you to see

calcium A mineral contained in bone that makes it hard

capillaries The smallest blood vessels. They let oxygen and nutrients move from the blood to other body cells, and move wastes out.

cells Small units that are the "building blocks" of the body

cerebellum The part of your brain where complicated movements are controlled

cerebral hemispheres The two halves of your brain. Each hemisphere has different jobs.

consumption Taking in

contract Shortening of a muscle, making it tense up

cramp A sharp pain in your muscles caused by lack of oxygen

dermis The deeper layer of skin underneath the epidermis

dissecting Cutting something up in order to study it

enamel The hardest substance in the body, which teeth are made of

epidermis The outer layer of the skin, which is constantly replaced

femur Thigh bone, the largest bone in the human body

gametes Sperm and egg cells

glands Organs that store chemicals for use in the body

glucose A type of sugar that comes from carbohydrate foods

hormones Chemicals that allow different parts of the body to communicate with each other

humid A high level of water in the atmosphere

immune Resistant to an infection or disease

Ligaments Slightly flexible tissue that connects different bones to each other, forming joints

Lymph Liquid that circulates through the lymphatic system

Lymphocytes White blood cells that fight off disease by making antibodies to kill bacteria or virus cells

Medulla The part of your brain that keeps the automatic body functions going

Microbes Tiny organisms made of a single cell

Mouth-to-mouth resuscitation Breathing into someone else's mouth to help them start breathing again if they have stopped

Nutrients Substances that provide what the body needs to grow and survive

Optical illusion Images that trick the brain into seeing something different from what is really there

Organs Collections of tissues that form a body part with a specific function

Phagocytes White blood cells that fight off disease by breaking down bacteria or virus cells

Pus A fluid formed in infected tissue

Reaction time The time between seeing or hearing a signal, and starting to move in response to it

Receptor cells Cells that receive chemical signals from elsewhere in the body

Reflexes Very fast reactions to potentially damaging events, which go straight to and from the spinal cord without involving the brain

Relax Lengthening of a muscle, reducing tension

Retina The part of the eye that detects light and on which an image forms

Sprinters Athletes who run extremely fast for short distances

Starch A carbohydrate made from glucose

Tendons Tissues that connect muscles to bones

Toxic Poisonous

Tracing paper Thin paper that you can see through and used to trace designs or pictures

Ultrasound High-pitched sounds that are above the human hearing range so can't be heard by humans

Umami A really savory flavor

Urea A toxic substance formed from the breakdown of protein. It is cleaned from the blood by the kidneys.

Veins Blood vessels that carry blood from around the body back to the heart

Villi Small finger-like projections that absorb nutrients from food as it passes through the small intestine

Virus A small infectious particle that reproduces itself inside the cells of living creatures

Index

Index

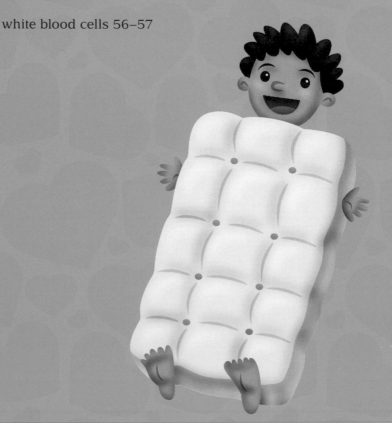